The MAJOR LEAGUE BASEBALL® BEST 50

Written by the Editors of Major League Baseball

MAJOR LEAGUE BASEBALL PROPERTIES, INC.

CONTENTS

The Major League Baseball Best 50 was developed, written and designed by MLB PUBLISHING, the publishing department of Major League Baseball Properties, Inc.

Printed in the U.S.A.

First Printing: June 2008

ISBN-13: 978-0-9776476-3-7

ISBN-10: 0-9776476-3-3

PHOTO CREDITS © MLB Photos Pilling (Rodriguez p. 4-5; Santana p. 7; Wright p. 8; Howard p. 10-11; Holliday p. 12; Ramirez p. 12; Rollins p. 12; Reyes p. 13; Beckett p. 14; Guerrero p. 15; Utley p. 15; Ichiro p. 16-17; Sizemore p. 19; Beltran p. 19; Sabathia p. 20; Papelbon p. 20; Fielder p. 21; Morneau p. 22; Verlander p. 22; Jeter p. 23; Soriano p. 24; Rivera p. 26; Griffey p. 27; Phillips p. 29; Hamels p. 32; Jones p. 33; Wells p. 33; Smoltz p. 34; Martin p. 34; Upton p. 35; Granderson p. 36-37; Papelbon p. 38; Wally p. 39; Wrigley Field p. 40; Ortiz p. 40; Reyes p. 41; Beltran p. 42; Helton p. 43). Cunningham (Martinez p. 26). Grieshop (Lee p. 33). Williamson (Ramirez p. 41). **© Getty Images** Robbins (Pujols p. 6). Jasenski (Peavy p. 7). Messerschmidt (Cabrera p. 8). Benc (Ramirez p. 9). Fiume (Webb p. 14; Crawford p. 20). Elsa (Ortiz p. 15; Berkman p. 24). Shamus (Ordonez p. 18). Hallowell (Teixeira p. 24). Daniel (Zambrano p. 25; Braun p. 29). Sandford (Halladay p. 25). Petersen (Rodriguez p. 26). Dunn (Oswalt p. 27). Schneider (Nathan p. 28). Gross (Haren p. 30-31). How (Owings p. 38). **© AP** Ruelas (Hunter p. 42).

There are 30 Major League teams, and more than 700 active players in the Big Leagues, but just nine can play on the field at once. And in *The Major League Baseball Best 50*, only one player can be No. 1. In fact, there can only be one No. 4, one No. 23 and one No. 45, too.

Baseball is and always has been about debating the value of a swing, a fastball, a player's range at short or his quickness down the line. Back in the 1920s, fans debated who was better: Babe Ruth or Ty Cobb? In the 1940s, you were a fan of either Ted Williams or Joe DiMaggio. During the 1980 World Series between the Royals and Phillies, all fans wanted to talk about was which team's third baseman was more impressive — George Brett or Mike Schmidt?

And the questions continue. How do today's players stack up? Who will you be talking about for years to come? Does Johan Santana rank higher than Josh Beckett? What about Ichiro vs. Curtis Granderson in center? Can Ryan Howard crank a ball farther than "Big Papi"?

Hopefully you'll spend plenty of time creating your own list, and watching your favorite players earn their way onto it. But what follows is our list. So turn the page and start comparing.

1 ALEX RODRIGUEZ

POSITION: THIRD BASE TEAM: NEW YORK YANKEES THROWS: RIGHT BATS: RIGHT UNIFORM #: 13

When A-Rod gets hot, there is no one better. Since making his Big League debut with Seattle as an 18-year-old shortstop in 1994, Alex has proven to be one of the game's greatest all-around players, and one of its most feared sluggers. In 2007, he became the youngest player ever to reach 500 home runs. He may have the largest contract in baseball history, but A-Rod still has that kid inside of him, the one who jumped up and down on the bed and hit his head on the ceiling when the ball went through Bill Buckner's legs in the 1986 World Series. "Why do I play baseball?" says the AL's 2003, 2005 and 2007 Most Valuable Player. "Because I love it. Making money doesn't mean your passion stops."

magic number

54

A-Rod's homers in 2007 — the most ever by a third baseman

factoid
As a kid, A-Rod was a big collector of baseball cards. So he was pretty thrilled when the Topps company asked him to be its first official spokesman in 2004.

2 ALBERT PUJOLS

POSITION: FIRST BASE TEAM: ST. LOUIS CARDINALS THROWS: RIGHT BATS: RIGHT UNIFORM #: 5

Albert Pujols doesn't need his own clothing line or a catchy nickname. His incredible skills alone have made him one of the most famous athletes on the planet. But it's his tireless work ethic and desire to constantly keep improving that have put him in a class by himself. Before turning 27, Pujols won Rookie of the Year, MVP and Gold Glove awards, a batting title and — most importantly — a World Series ring. Since coming to America from the Dominican Republic when he was a young boy, Pujols has dedicated himself to being the best he can be both on and off the field. "I think he distinguishes himself every day," says Cardinals Manager Tony La Russa.

stat chart

Albert's first seven seasons have been incredible. Here's how they compare to two all-time greats:
ALBERT PUJOLS (2001–07):
.332 AVG, 282 HR, 861 RBI
JOE DiMAGGIO (1936–42):
.339 AVG, 219 HR, 930 RBI
TED WILLIAMS (1939–42, 46–48):
.354 AVG, 222 HR, 879 RBI

3 JOHAN SANTANA

POSITION: PITCHER
TEAM: NEW YORK METS
THROWS: LEFT
BATS: LEFT
UNIFORM #: 57

It's hard to believe that not one, but two teams passed on Johan Santana early in his career. After he signed with Houston in 1995, Florida picked him up virtually free of charge in the 1999 Rule 5 Draft and dealt him to the Twins. Johan then gave eight years of unstoppable performances in Minnesota before he was traded to the Mets in 2008. The Venezuelan left-hander won his second Cy Young Award in 2006 — the only pitcher in Twins history with more than one. With a mid-90s fastball and mid-70s change-up, Santana can fool even the best hitters. "He is the best pitcher in the game," says Frank Thomas.

4 JAKE PEAVY

POSITION: PITCHER
TEAM: SAN DIEGO PADRES
THROWS: RIGHT
BATS: RIGHT
UNIFORM #: 44

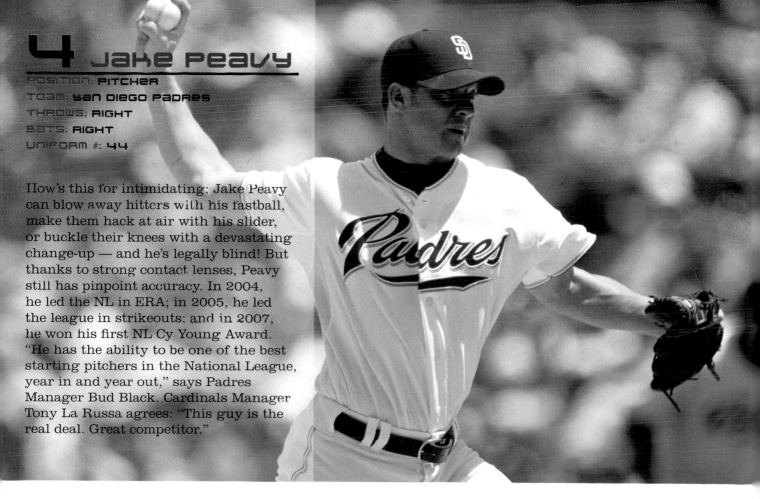

How's this for intimidating: Jake Peavy can blow away hitters with his fastball, make them hack at air with his slider, or buckle their knees with a devastating change-up — and he's legally blind! But thanks to strong contact lenses, Peavy still has pinpoint accuracy. In 2004, he led the NL in ERA; in 2005, he led the league in strikeouts; and in 2007, he won his first NL Cy Young Award. "He has the ability to be one of the best starting pitchers in the National League, year in and year out," says Padres Manager Bud Black. Cardinals Manager Tony La Russa agrees: "This guy is the real deal. Great competitor."

5 DAVID WRIGHT

POSITION: THIRD BASE
TEAM: NEW YORK METS
THROWS: RIGHT
BATS: RIGHT
UNIFORM #: 5

When the Mets drafted David Wright out of Hickory (Va.) High School in 2001, they got more than just a talented infielder who could hit home runs and drive in more than 100 runs every year. They got a young player capable of being a true team leader — that rare guy who can lift a team's spirits when the going gets tough. "I can't say enough good things about him," says former teammate Joe McEwing. "He works hard every single day, and whatever he gets, he deserves."

"I played against David Wright at every level in the Minors. I'm a little nervous.
—Ryan Howard on facing Wright in the 2006 Home Run Derby"

6 MIGUEL CABRERA

POSITION: FIRST BASE
TEAM: DETROIT TIGERS
THROWS: RIGHT
BATS: RIGHT
UNIFORM #: 24

Cabrera made his debut in June of 2003 at the age of 20. Four months later, he was a world champion with the Marlins. In the four seasons that followed, Cabrera averaged more than 26 home runs and 112 RBI. "He's so advanced and disciplined for a hitter at his young age," says Mets third baseman David Wright. "He has tormented us every time we've played him." Fortunately for Wright and the rest of the National League, Cabrera left the NL and moved north to Detroit in 2008, where he transitioned across the diamond to first base.

7 HANLEY RAMIREZ

POSITION: SHORTSTOP TEAM: FLORIDA MARLINS THROWS: RIGHT BATS: RIGHT UNIFORM #: 2

Hanley Ramirez has a solid mix of speed and power. As a rookie in 2006, he stole 51 bases, hit 17
homers and was named NL Rookie of the Year. He was the first NL rookie ever to record more than 50
steals and 110 runs, and followed it up with another stellar performance, stealing another 51 bases
and scoring 125 times in '07. "He has the opportunity to be a complete player," says Dodgers coach
Mariano Duncan, who first saw Hanley play a few years ago in the Dominican Republic. "Very few
shortstops in this day have the speed he has and the power he has, with the ability to hit for average.
In two or three years, you'll see him in that group with Derek Jeter and Miguel Tejada."

8 RYAN HOWARD

POSITION: FIRST BASE TEAM: PHILADELPHIA PHILLIES THROWS: LEFT BATS: LEFT UNIFORM #: 6

After winning Minor League MVP awards in 2003 and '04, Ryan Howard became the target of several teams looking to trade for him. Luckily for the Phillies, they held on to their supersized slugger and have been greatly rewarded. Howard was the NL Rookie of the Year in 2005, and took home MVP honors in '06 — the first player since Cal Ripken to win those two awards in his first two seasons. His terrific 2006 season was highlighted by 58 homers — the most ever for a second-year player — and in '07 he kept his momentum, driving in 136 runs with a .584 slugging percentage.

factoid

From Sept. 17 to Sept. 30 of 2007, in the final 13 games of the regular season, Ryan produced nine home runs and 21 RBI.

10

"He's got so much opposite-field power. Not many guys can go opposite field with that kind of power. —Chase Utley"

9 MATT HOLLIDAY

POSITION: LEFT FIELD
TEAM: COLORADO ROCKIES
THROWS: RIGHT
BATS: RIGHT
UNIFORM #: 5

After just three seasons, Matt Holliday was already a Big League star. The most impressive thing about him, though, was how much he improved every year. Matt had a solid rookie season in 2004, hitting .290 with 14 homers. The next year, his numbers went up in every category, and then again in 2006, when his average jumped 19 points to .326 and he hit 15 more longballs. But his '07 campaign was a true coming-out party; he raked 36 homers and hit .340 to take the NL batting title. Now everyone is taking notice.

10 MANNY RAMIREZ

POSITION: LEFT FIELD
TEAM: BOSTON RED SOX
THROWS: RIGHT
BATS: RIGHT
UNIFORM #: 24

In his second-ever Big League game, Manny Ramirez hit two home runs at Yankee Stadium, and he's been going deep ever since, approaching his 500th homer at the start of 2008. From 1995 to 2007, he hit more than 30 longballs 11 times, drove in more than 100 runs 11 times and played on 10 All-Star teams. Manny has a style that's all his own — guarding Fenway's Green Monster unlike your "typical" ballplayer. But when you put up numbers like he has, any team would be happy to have him. The 2004 World Series MVP and 2007 world champion is also second on the all-time grand slams list.

11 JIMMY ROLLINS

POSITION: SHORTSTOP
TEAM: PHILADELPHIA PHILLIES
THROWS: RIGHT
BATS: SWITCH
UNIFORM #: 11

Even on an infield with Chase Utley and Ryan Howard, Rollins gets noticed plenty. That's because he's a talented, fun-to-watch player. Before the 2007 season, he got people talking when he said his Phillies were the team to beat in the NL East. It was a bold thing to say, but it helped get Philadelphia excited enough to finish in first place for the first time since 1993. And Jimmy did his part to make it come true, too. He tallied 30 homers, 38 doubles and 20 triples, while driving in 94 runs and stealing 41 bases. And the 2007 NL MVP shows no signs of slowing down.

12 JOSE REYES

POSITION: SHORTSTOP TEAM: NEW YORK METS THROWS: RIGHT BATS: SWITCH UNIFORM #: 7

Major Leaguers are fans, too, and if you ask them what player they would pay to see, their answer is almost always the same: Jose Reyes. The speedy leadoff man dazzles on the diamond, turning doubles into triples, stealing bases (he set a single-season franchise record in 2007 with 78 stolen bases) and scoring runs. Usually, when he is thriving, the Mets are, too. Conversely, when he slumps, the rest of the team suffers. Thanks to his unbelievable range and strong arm, Reyes also is one of the game's best shortstops. "The guy who can take over the game the fastest is Jose Reyes," says former teammate Paul Lo Duca. "He's the most exciting player, and he can be dominant."

stat chart
Here's how Jose's first five seasons compare to those of another great leadoff hitter, Rickey Henderson:
REYES (2003–07):
420 R, 52 3B, 234 SB
HENDERSON (1979–83):
473 R, 25 3B, 427 SB

13 JOSH BECKETT

POSITION: PITCHER
TEAM: BOSTON RED SOX
THROWS: RIGHT
BATS: RIGHT
UNIFORM #: 19

Josh Beckett was locked in right out of the gate in 2007, starting 10-1 with a 3.14 ERA in 13 starts and helping the Red Sox take a comfortable lead in the AL East. His dominance lasted to the end, pushing Boston to its second world championship in four years, as he was the only Major League pitcher to win 20 games that season. Now Beckett's got the talent, the experience (he also sparked the Marlins to a World Series title in 2003) and the confidence to remain one of the best pitchers for years to come.

factoid

In his senior year of high school, Beckett went 10-1 with an 0.46 ERA. He also was named USA Today's High School Pitcher of the Year.

14 BRANDON WEBB

POSITION: PITCHER
TEAM: ARIZONA DIAMONDBACKS
THROWS: RIGHT
BATS: RIGHT
UNIFORM #: 17

You step back into the batter's box to face Brandon Webb. Your knees are shaking. He has you down 0-2 and you're just looking for something to hit. His next pitch looks like a strike, but just as you bring the bat around, the ball drops to the dirt. It's too late to stop your swing, so the ball dribbles out to the mound for an easy putout. Don't feel too bad, though. Nearly nine out of 10 Big Leaguers make an out in an 0-2 count against Webb. That sinker is often called one of the game's very best pitches. It helped Webb earn the NL Cy Young Award in 2006, and win 18 games — with a 3.01 ERA and 194 strikeouts — in 2007.

15 VLaDIMIR GUeRReRo

POSITION: RIGHT FIELD TEAM: LOS ANGELES ANGELS OF ANAHEIM
THROWS: RIGHT BATS: RIGHT UNIFORM #: 27

Vladi has been punishing AL pitchers for so long some people forget he was a four-time All-Star with the Montreal Expos. But all it takes is one game to remember just how dominant he can be. Able to crush almost any pitch remotely near the strike zone, the 2004 AL MVP has never hit below .302 in a full season or slugged below .547 since he came to the Angels in 2005. Former teammate Darin Erstad put it best: "He's one of those guys that you're going to tell your grandkids about."

16 DaVID ORTIZ

POSITION: DESIGNATED HITTER TEAM: BOSTON RED SOX
THROWS: LEFT BATS: LEFT UNIFORM #: 34

Since joining the Red Sox in 2003, "Big Papi" has become one of baseball's offensive masters. He blasted 11 walk-off homers in his first five seasons in Boston, plus two in the 2004 playoffs. "When you can come through in those situations, people really appreciate it," says the two-time world champion. "It takes a lot of concentration. I guess it's been working the right way for me, and I'm going to try to keep it that way."

17 CHaSe UTLeY

POSITION: SECOND BASE
TEAM: PHILADELPHIA PHILLIES
THROWS: RIGHT
BATS: LEFT
UNIFORM #: 26

Utley's first Big League hit was a grand slam, a fitting way for the Phillies' star second baseman to start his career. Originally sharing time with Placido Polanco, Utley didn't disappoint when he was given the full-time starting job. In 2006 — just his second full season in the Majors — he scored the most runs in the NL (131). Chase was voted to the All-Star Game as the NL's starting second baseman that year and won his first Silver Slugger Award. He kept up the pace in 2007, and won his second Silver Slugger Award, going on to tie a franchise record in 2008 by hitting a home run in five straight games.

18 ICHIRO SUZUKI

POSITION: CENTER FIELD TEAM: SEATTLE MARINERS THROWS: RIGHT BATS: LEFT UNIFORM #: 51

After winning seven consecutive batting titles and Gold Glove Awards in Japan, Ichiro became the first Japanese position player to sign with a Major League club. In 2001, his combination of speed, instincts and overall skills led him to become the second player ever to win Rookie of the Year and MVP honors in the same season in 2001. "He can hit anything," says Yankees southpaw Andy Pettitte. "You just have to hope he hits it up in the air, because he's so fast that he beats out ground balls." In his first seven Big League seasons, Ichiro won seven Gold Gloves and made seven All-Star teams. In 2004, he set a single-season record with 262 hits. By April 2008, he had surpassed the 1,600-hit plateau.

magic number

45

**Ichiro's consecutive steals from
4/29/2006 to 5/16/2007, an AL record**

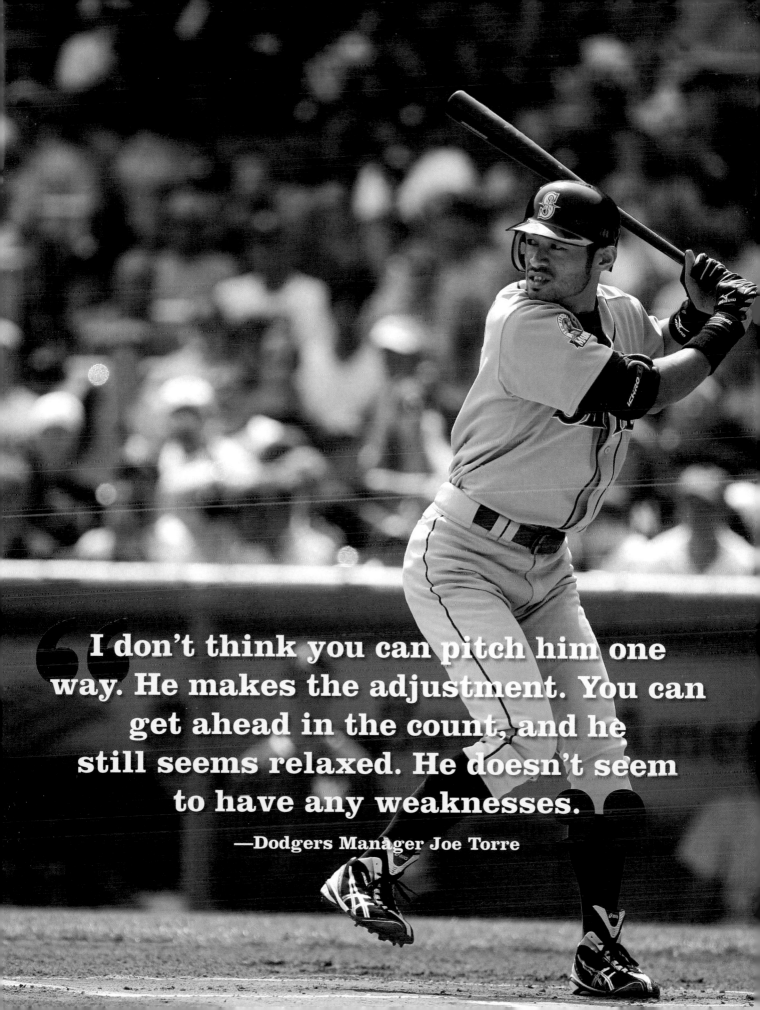

"I don't think you can pitch him one way. He makes the adjustment. You can get ahead in the count, and he still seems relaxed. He doesn't seem to have any weaknesses.

—Dodgers Manager Joe Torre

19 MAGGLIO ORDONEZ

POSITION: RIGHT FIELD TEAM: DETROIT TIGERS THROWS: RIGHT BATS: RIGHT UNIFORM #: 30

After several spectacular seasons with the Chicago White Sox, in which he made four All-Star teams, Tigers outfielder Magglio Ordonez suffered through two injury-plagued seasons before roaring back in his second campaign with Detroit in 2006. That year, Maggs helped lead the Tigers to their first World Series appearance in 22 years by knocking in a team-leading 104 runs. He followed up that year with the type of season that would normally lead to a MVP Award were it not for the tremendous year that New York's Alex Rodriguez had. In 2007, Ordonez won the batting title with a .363 average and posted a career-high 139 RBI.

stat chart

Magglio has averaged stellar stats since his debut in 1997:

HITS: 150

RBI: 90

HOME RUNS: 23

AVG: .312

OPS: .892

20 GRADY SIZEMORE

POSITION: CENTER FIELD
TEAM: CLEVELAND INDIANS
THROWS: LEFT
BATS: LEFT
UNIFORM #: 24

Whether the Indians are ahead or behind, heading toward the playoffs or heading home, Grady Sizemore plays the same way every day: with 100 percent, all-out effort. He'll routinely crash into walls to catch fly balls or turn on the afterburners to beat out infield grounders in meaningless games. Thanks to Sizemore, though, Cleveland won't be playing many of those. In 2006, the Washington native became the youngest player in history with 90 extra-base hits and 20 steals in the same year. And in 2007, his bat helped lead the Indians deep into the postseason, with an OPS of 1.212 during the ALDS.

21 CARLOS BELTRAN

POSITION: CENTER FIELD
TEAM: NEW YORK METS
THROWS: RIGHT
BATS: SWITCH
UNIFORM #: 15

From the graceful way he covers the outfield to his sweet, powerful swing at the plate, Carlos Beltran makes it look so easy. "He can do a little bit of everything," says former teammate Tom Glavine. The Mets signed Beltran as a free agent after his stellar performance in the 2004 playoffs with Houston, when he hit eight homers in 12 games. He has been a great contributor in New York, too — he hit three homers in the '06 NLCS and was elected to 2007's All-Star roster.

"Honestly, I think that Carlos being labeled as a 30/30 guy might be a bit of an understatement. —David Wright"

22 C.C. SABATHIA

POSITION: PITCHER

TEAM: CLEVELAND INDIANS

THROWS: LEFT

BATS: LEFT

UNIFORM #: 52

Weighing in at 290 pounds, the 6-foot-7 C.C. Sabathia is the heaviest player in the Majors, but he hasn't let the weight of expectations as a former first-round draft pick become too burdensome. Since he made his debut in 2001, Sabathia has proven to be one of the game's most durable pitchers, reaching at least 30 starts in six of his first seven Major League seasons. The three-time All-Star had a tremendous season in 2007, when he recorded career bests in innings pitched (241), wins (19), strikeouts (209), and ERA (3.21), leading to his first Cy Young Award. He also helped Cleveland get within one game of the World Series.

23 CARL CRAWFORD

POSITION: LEFT FIELD

TEAM: TAMPA BAY RAYS

THROWS: LEFT

BATS: LEFT

UNIFORM #: 13

The Rays knew Crawford was multi-talented when they drafted him out of high school in 1999. What the team didn't expect was how much he would improve. He is just the second player ever to increase his batting average in six straight seasons and home run total in five straight seasons. He's on pace to join Ty Cobb and reach 1,000 hits, 300 steals and 100 triples before he turns 28.

24 JONATHAN PAPELBON

POSITION: PITCHER

TEAM: BOSTON RED SOX

THROWS: RIGHT

BATS: RIGHT

UNIFORM #: 58

In 2006, Jonathan Papelbon was off the charts as the full-time closer. He recorded 20 straight saves in the team's first 52 games and allowed just seven earned runs all season in 59 appearances. "The fact that he can throw any of his pitches behind in the count ... and is a guy with a 97-98 mph fastball," says Phillies pitcher Tom Gordon, "he's going to be tough to beat. He can only get better, and with what he's doing now, can you imagine that?" The '07 season was similar, as Papelbon completed 37 of 40 save opportunities with an ERA of 1.85, and took the momentum into '08, with 10 saves in his first 10 chances.

25 PRINCE FIELDER

POSITION: FIRST BASE TEAM: MILWAUKEE BREWERS THROWS: RIGHT BATS: LEFT UNIFORM #: 28

Prince Fielder may have sworn off meat, but his appetite for the longball will never be satisfied. Ever since he was a kid, he's had a knack for crushing baseballs, as he often could be seen hitting home runs in batting practice at Tiger Stadium, where his father, Cecil, used to play as a member of the Tigers. As a 22-year-old rookie in 2005, Fielder leapt onto the MLB scene by hitting 28 out of the park, and just a year later he became the youngest player in MLB history to hit 50 home runs in a season. The Brewers, who haven't reached the postseason in more than two decades, plan to ride Fielder's massive shoulders to future success.

factoid

Prince and his dad, Cecil, are the only father-son combination in baseball history to hit 50 home runs in a season. (Cecil hit 51 in 1990.)

26 JUSTIN MORNEAU

POSITION: FIRST BASE
TEAM: MINNESOTA TWINS
THROWS: RIGHT
BATS: LEFT
UNIFORM #: 33

One of the latest stars to come out of Minnesota's terrific Minor League system, Morneau was drafted by the Twins in 1999. After playing in the Majors a bit in 2003, he got more playing time in 2004 and 2005, but really took off in 2006. Morneau hit .321 with 34 homers and 130 RBI to help the Twins win the AL Central that year. For his efforts, he was named AL MVP, making him the first Canadian to receive that honor. In 2007 he showed no sign of stopping, adding 31 home runs, 111 RBI and a career-high 64 walks to his already stellar stats.

27 JUSTIN VERLANDER

POSITION: PITCHER TEAM: DETROIT TIGERS THROWS: RIGHT BATS: RIGHT UNIFORM #: 35

Twenty-five years old and with just two full seasons of Big League experience under his belt, Justin Verlander has already become the unquestioned leader of the Detroit Tigers' pitching staff. Armed with a 100-mph fastball, the 6-foot-5 flamethrower has been wowing fans with radar gun readings, and intimidating hitters since his AL Rookie of the Year campaign in 2006. After helping the Tigers reach the World Series that year, the Virginia native threw even better in 2007, striking out 59 more batters than he did in the previous season. He also pitched a no-hitter on June 12, the first ever at Detroit's Comerica Park, and made his first All-Star Game appearance.

28 DEREK JETER

POSITION: SHORTSTOP TEAM: NEW YORK YANKEES THROWS: RIGHT BATS: RIGHT UNIFORM #: 2

When Derek Jeter's career comes to an end, there will be countless ways of recognizing what a great player he was. But to measure Jeter's full value, you have to look beyond awards and statistics. "He can do it all," says fellow perennial All-Star Ichiro Suzuki. "There is no one part of his game you can focus on stopping." When Alex Rodriguez joined the Yankees in 2004, he said, "Derek does it all with grace and elegance." His smooth defense, his knack for coming up big when it counts and his leadership on and off the field all ensure that the Yankee captain's legacy will last forever.

"Being a leader is not something I think about. I try to lead by example, by playing hard. —Derek Jeter"

29 ALFONSO SORIANO

POSITION: OUTFIELD
TeaM: CHICAGO CUBS
THROWS: RIGHT
BATS: RIGHT
UNIFORM #: 12

Lou Piniella has managed some great players, including A-Rod, Ken Griffey Jr. and Carl Crawford. Now, as manager of the Cubs, he gets to work with another great talent: Alfonso Soriano. "I mean this guy here has got just a special combination of speed and power," Piniella says. That was true for sure in '06, when Soriano became the first ever to hit 40 homers, 40 doubles and steal 40 bases in the same season. Coming from a humble background, though, he never forgets his roots. "Everything I do in baseball is dedicated to my mother back in the Dominican Republic," he says.

30 Lance Berkman

POSITION: FIRST BASE   TeaM: HOUSTON ASTROS
THROWS: LEFT   BATS: SWITCH   UNIFORM #: 17

Whether he is playing the outfield, where he spent most of his time early in his career, or at first base, where he plays most often these days, Lance Berkman can swing the bat. On Sept. 13, 2006, he became just the second switch-hitter in history to hit 40 or more home runs in multiple seasons, joining Mickey Mantle, appropriately. "My dad was a Yankees fan," Lance says, "and he wanted me to be a switch-hitter because Mickey Mantle was his favorite player."

31 MARK TEIXEIRA

POSITION: FIRST BASE   TeaM: ATLANTA BRAVES   THROWS: RIGHT
BATS: SWITCH   UNIFORM #: 24

A late July '07 trade to Atlanta boosted Teixeira's late-season stats and cemented his value to the Braves. But success is nothing new to the first baseman. After a stellar rookie season in 2003, Teixeira wasn't content. He continued to work hard on all aspects of his game. "I go out there and expect a lot out of myself," he says. Thanks to the effort, he had at least 30 homers and more than 100 RBI in each of the next four seasons, and won Gold Gloves in 2005 and 2006.

Factoid
When he was taken by the Texas Rangers with the fifth pick of the 2001 Draft, Mark was the first of nine Georgia Tech players chosen that year.

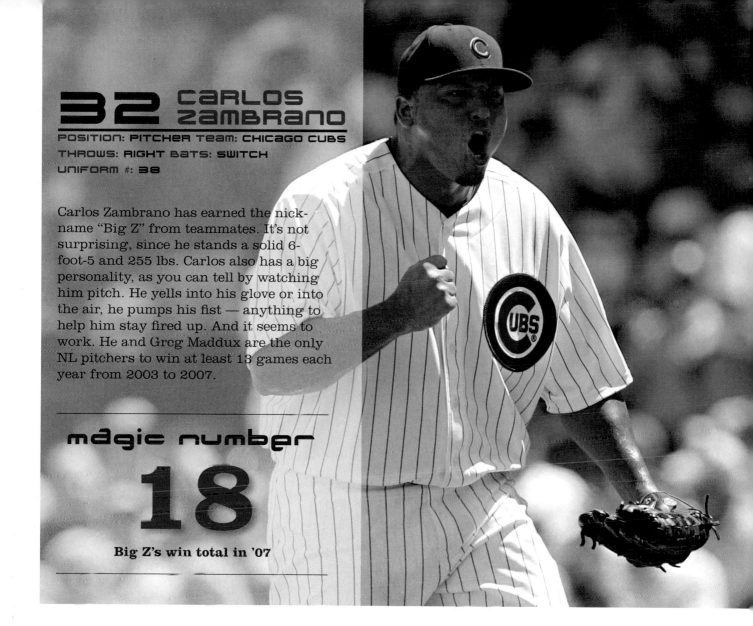

32 CARLOS ZAMBRANO

POSITION: PITCHER TEAM: CHICAGO CUBS
THROWS: RIGHT BATS: SWITCH
UNIFORM #: 38

Carlos Zambrano has earned the nickname "Big Z" from teammates. It's not surprising, since he stands a solid 6-foot-5 and 255 lbs. Carlos also has a big personality, as you can tell by watching him pitch. He yells into his glove or into the air, he pumps his fist — anything to help him stay fired up. And it seems to work. He and Greg Maddux are the only NL pitchers to win at least 13 games each year from 2003 to 2007.

magic number

18

Big Z's win total in '07

33 ROY HALLADAY

POSITION: PITCHER TEAM: TORONTO BLUE JAYS
THROWS: RIGHT BATS: RIGHT UNIFORM #: 32

After being drafted out of Arvada (Colo.) West High School in 1995, Roy Halladay was called up at the end of the 1998 season and soon showed the Blue Jays just what kind of pitcher they had. In his second career start, he had a no-hitter going until a pinch-hitter homered with two outs in the ninth. Halladay hung on for the complete-game victory that day — a stat that would become his trademark. "Doc," as he is known, works quickly and isn't afraid to go all nine. Of his 22 wins in 2003, when he won the AL Cy Young Award, eight were complete games (and he had another seven last year, tops in the Bigs). In 2008, 10 years after his impressive Big League debut, he became the first pitcher in Blue Jays' history to make six straight Opening Day starts.

34 MARIANO RIVERA

POSITION: PITCHER
TEAM: NEW YORK YANKEES
THROWS: RIGHT
BATS: RIGHT
UNIFORM #: 42

Regarded by many as the greatest relief pitcher to ever play, Mariano Rivera has dominated hitters ever since becoming the Yankees' full-time closer back in 1997. While he averages more than 40 saves per year during the regular season, reaching a total of 450 in late April of 2008, Rivera shines his brightest under the intense pressure of the playoffs. Through 2007, Mo had recorded a 0.77 ERA and 34 saves (19 more than the next closest guy, Dennis Eckersley) in postseason play — both of which are Major League records.

factoid

The only player who wears No. 42 regularly, Rivera is the last player who will ever wear the number since it was retired in 1997 as a tribute to Jackie Robinson.

35 FRANCISCO RODRIGUEZ

POSITION: PITCHER
TEAM: LOS ANGELES ANGELS OF ANAHEIM
THROWS: RIGHT
BATS: RIGHT
UNIFORM #: 57

His nickname is K-Rod (and it's not because of a love for Special K cereal). Francisco Rodriguez, the closer for the Los Angeles Angels of Anaheim, strikes people out in bunches. Entering 2008, he had five straight seasons with 90 or more Ks, thanks to a blazing fastball and sharp slider. Such terrific stuff has also meant loads of saves for Rodriguez and loads of wins for the Angels. On Sept. 10, 2006, at age 24, K-Rod became the youngest pitcher ever to reach the 100-save mark. Since Rodriguez's debut in 2002, the Angels have been to the playoffs four times and won a World Series.

36 VICTOR MARTINEZ

POSITION: CATCHER/FIRST BASE
TEAM: CLEVELAND INDIANS
THROWS: RIGHT
BATS: SWITCH
UNIFORM #: 41

When a catcher can don heavy equipment daily and wield a hot bat at the plate, everyone takes notice. After dominating in the Minors, Venezuelan-born Victor Martinez (called up in 2002) earned the starting job going into his first full season with the Indians, and switch-hit his way onto the AL All-Star team. In 2006, an effort to keep V-Mart's bat in the lineup made Cleveland Manager Eric Wedge play him at first base as well. And, to the dismay of opposing pitchers, it worked. In 2007 Martinez was fresh come October, when he batted a combined average of .318 in two playoff series.

37 ROY OSWALT

POSITION: PITCHER
TEAM: HOUSTON ASTROS
THROWS: RIGHT
BATS: RIGHT
UNIFORM #: 44

Like Nolan Ryan and Roger Clemens, Roy Oswalt has had terrific seasons in Houston. But when it comes to being a star, Oswalt prefers to stay out of the spotlight. "He just likes going out and pitching, doing his job and saying 'Thank you very much' and going on home," says former Astros Manager Phil Garner. But that doesn't mean the quiet Mississippian isn't a bulldog on the mound. In 2005, Oswalt became the first Astro in 25 years to post back-to-back 20-win seasons, and he helped Houston reach its first World Series.

"**Anyone who's around [Griffey] sees that he hits and hits and hits. I don't know how he does it.** —former teammate Austin Kearns"

38 KEN GRIFFEY JR.

POSITION: RIGHT FIELD **TEAM:** CINCINNATI REDS
THROWS: LEFT **BATS:** LEFT **UNIFORM #:** 3

"Player of the '90s" — that's a title that just one man can put on his resume: Ken Griffey Jr. Throughout the decade, Griffey played incredible baseball, both at the plate and in center field, taking the AL MVP Award in 1997. While Junior has had a tough time battling injuries in this decade, he is still capable of taking a pitcher deep and driving in plenty of runs. With a trophy case full of Gold Glove Awards to prove his value in the field, and a position among the likes of Babe Ruth, Hank Aaron and Willie Mays by going after his 600th home run in 2008, Griffey seems a lock for the Hall of Fame. And with his outgoing personality and constant smile, Junior will always be a favorite among fans and teammates.

39 Joe nathan

POSITION: PITCHER TEAM: MINNESOTA TWINS THROWS: RIGHT BATS: RIGHT UNIFORM #: 36

Joe Nathan was traded to the Twins from San Francisco before the 2004 season. As a Giant, Nathan never had a real chance to close games and he recorded just one save in four years there. A few seasons later, thanks to his opportunity in Minnesota, he has become one of the best closers in baseball. He saved 44 games in his first year in Minnesota (in just 47 chances), and 116 over the next three years. And since moving to the AL, he has kept his ERA below 3.00. Nathan's pretty smart, too. In 1997, he graduated from SUNY Stony Brook, where he was a two-time Academic All-American.

40 BRANDON PHILLIPS

POSITION: SECOND BASE
TEAM: CINCINNATI REDS
THROWS: RIGHT
BATS: RIGHT
UNIFORM #: 4

On Aug. 1, 2007, Brandon Phillips stole two bases on a single pitch against the Nationals. And that was only the second-most amazing thing the second baseman did that season. With 30 longballs and 32 stolen bases, the Reds star became just the second member of an exclusive second baseman's club. He joined Alfonso Soriano as one of the only two players at the position ever to go for 30 and 30 in a single season. Phillips — who was a two-sport star (he also excelled in football) in high school — had a breakout season in 2007, finishing in the top 10 in the NL in runs, singles, stolen bases and at-bats. This has made him a popular player for both the Reds and fantasy baseball team owners.

41 RYAN BRAUN

POSITION: LEFT FIELD
TEAM: MILWAUKEE BREWERS
THROWS: RIGHT
BATS: RIGHT
UNIFORM #: 8

Not only was Ryan Braun the Rookie of the Year in his debut campaign, but he also hit 34 home runs (fifth best in the NL) en route to breaking Mark McGwire's Big League rookie slugging record. A No. 5 overall pick in 2005 by the Brewers, Braun was a terror in the Minors before coming up in May '07. He adds another power bat to the Brewers' lineup, which already features slugger and fellow *MLB Best 50* man Prince Fielder. We think Braun will be battling his bigger teammate for the home run crown for many more years.

42 DAN HAREN

POSITION: PITCHER
TEAM: ARIZONA DIAMONDBACKS
THROWS: RIGHT
BATS: RIGHT
UNIFORM #: 15

Although he went from starting for the American League in the 2007 All-Star Game to playing the role of Robin to the D-backs' Batman — Brandon Webb — Dan Haren won't be complaining because he's part of the National League's best 1-2 pitching combination. Always at home on the mound, the right-handed California native takes the ball from his manager every fifth game and mows down opposing hitters wherever he is in the rotation. He started 34 games each year from 2005 through 2007 and set career highs in wins, strikeouts (192) and ERA last year. With a split-finger fastball that plummets just as it reaches the strike zone, batters are at his mercy.

> " We were all impressed with his competitiveness, his toughness; obviously his stuff. So we had big plans for his future. "
>
> —2007 NL All-Star Manager Tony La Russa

magic number

15

Haren's team-leading win total in
2007, a career-high

43 COLE HAMELS

POSITION: PITCHER TEAM: PHILADELPHIA PHILLIES THROWS: LEFT BATS: LEFT UNIFORM #: 35

After overcoming more than a fair share of injuries during his Minor League days, Cole Hamels, or "Hollywood" as his Phillies teammates call him, has become one of the Major Leagues' most lethal southpaws. Finally healthy, Hamels has been heating up the rotation ever since he was called up to Philly in 2006. And he didn't waste any time, throwing five scoreless innings and allowing just one hit in his Big League debut on May 12. Hamels was selected to the NL All-Star team in 2007, his first complete campaign in the Major Leagues, and led his team in wins (15), ERA (3.39, the lowest among all starting pitchers) and strikeouts (177) on the season.

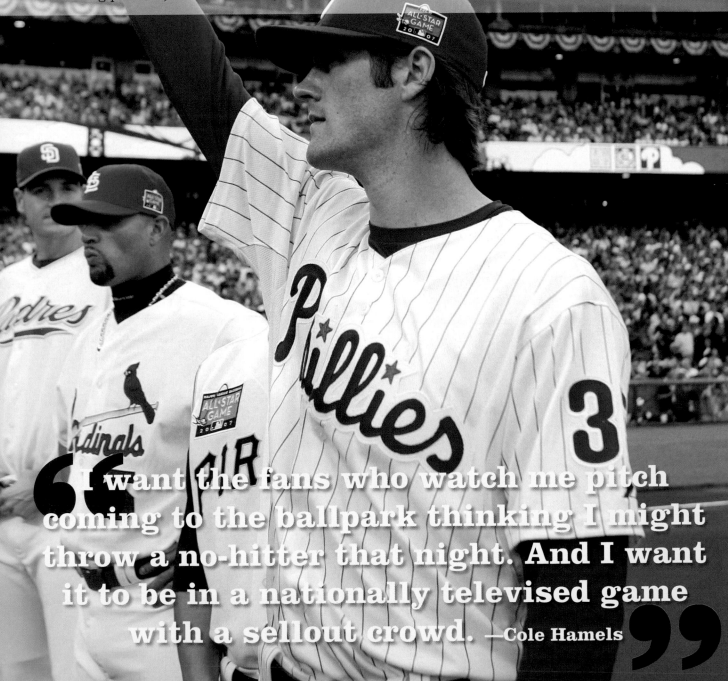

" I want the fans who watch me pitch coming to the ballpark thinking I might throw a no-hitter that night. And I want it to be in a nationally televised game with a sellout crowd. —Cole Hamels **"**

44 CHIPPER JONES

POSITION: THIRD BASE TEAM: ATLANTA BRAVES
THROWS: RIGHT BATS: SWITCH UNIFORM #: 10

Chipper Jones became a Brave when Atlanta drafted him No. 1 overall in the 1990 amateur draft, and has been notably consistent since his rookie season in 1995. He has hit at least 20 home runs every year, finishing with more than 100 RBI nine times. Chipper has also compiled a career OBP of more than .400, which ranks him on the all-time top 50 list. At 36, the 1999 NL MVP kept it hot in 2008 batting .422 with a 1.171 OPS in April.

45 VERNON WELLS

POSITION: CENTER FIELD TEAM: TORONTO BLUE JAYS
THROWS: RIGHT BATS: RIGHT UNIFORM #: 10

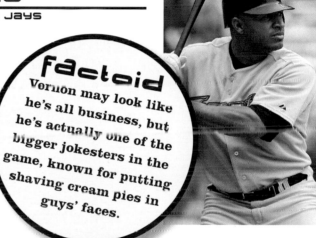

One day during Little League practice, a ground ball smacked young Vernon Wells in the face. After that, he decided to give the outfield a try, and that decision eventually made him a Big League All-Star. In 2004, Wells played 130 games in center field for the Blue Jays, making just one error and winning his first Gold Glove. The next year, he played in 153 games without a single error! Vernon is more than just a slick fielder — in 2003, he led the Majors with 215 hits.

factoid Vernon may look like he's all business, but he's actually one of the bigger jokesters in the game, known for putting shaving cream pies in guys' faces.

46 CARLOS LEE

POSITION: LEFT FIELD
TEAM: HOUSTON ASTROS
THROWS: RIGHT
BATS: RIGHT
UNIFORM #: 45

The left fielder dubbed "El Caballo," ("The Horse" in Spanish) has been on a tear as hot as anyone's during the past five seasons. The Panamanian-born slugger began 2008 having smacked more than 30 homers, stolen 10 or more bases and played in more than 150 games in each of the last five years. Despite such gaudy numbers, the three-time All-Star and two-time Silver Slugger Award winner gets less attention than some of his big bopping peers. After he hit a homer in his debut at-bat (with the White Sox), "El Caballo" has shown teammates and fans in Houston that they can ride him to victory.

stat chart

Since 2002, Smoltz has been a star as a starter and a reliever.

	W	L	Saves	ERA
2002	3	2	55	3.25
2003	0	2	45	1.12
2004	0	1	44	2.76
	W	L	IP	ERA
2005	14	7	229.7	3.06
2006	16	9	232.0	3.49
2007	14	8	205.7	3.11

47 JOHN SMOLTZ

POSITION: PITCHER TEAM: ATLANTA BRAVES THROWS: RIGHT BATS: RIGHT UNIFORM #: 29

The Braves are fortunate to have John Smoltz — because he can excel both as a starting pitcher and as a reliever. He went 24-8 as a starter in 1996 and won the NL Cy Young Award. In 1995, he won 12 games, helping the Braves win the World Series. Years later, when Atlanta needed a closer, Smoltz took the job and did not miss a beat. He saved an NL-record 55 games in 2002 and won the Rolaids Relief Man Award. At age 41, he's still going strong, whether he's starting or coming out of the bullpen. On April 22, 2008, the likely future Hall of Famer became just the 16th MLB pitcher to strike out his 3,000th batter.

48 RUSSELL MARTIN

POSITION: CATCHER TEAM: LOS ANGELES DODGERS
THROWS: RIGHT BATS: RIGHT UNIFORM #: 55

A catcher must have a unique set of skills, and he needs to be tough enough to handle the physical demands of the position. Since switching from third base in the Minor Leagues, catching has fit Russell Martin like a glove. He made his Dodgers debut in 2006, and his star is still rising. He started for the 2007 NL All-Star team — the first Canadian catcher ever to do that — and won a Gold Glove for defensive excellence and a Silver Slugger as the NL's best-hitting catcher. Russell led all Big League catchers in stolen bases in 2007, too, the same year the Dodgers gave him the Roy Campanella Award as the team's most inspirational player. Is there anything he can't do?

magic number

.508

B.J.'s slugging percentage in 2007

49 B.J. UPTON

POSITION: CENTER FIELD TEAM: TAMPA BAY RAYS THROWS: RIGHT BATS: RIGHT UNIFORM #: 2

B.J., short for Bossman Junior (the original Bossman is his dad, Manny), certainly lives up to the name, patrolling center field for the Tampa Bay Rays like a seasoned pro. Upton was just 19 years old — and a middle infielder — when he broke into the Big Leagues on August 2, 2004. But with great athleticism and range, the Norfolk, Virginia native took easily to the outfield in early 2007. And he has been thriving there ever since. That year, his first full campaign in the Majors, he batted .300 and posted an OPS of .894, third in the Major Leagues among center fielders. Having made his Major League debut in the same year as other *MLB Best 50* stars Curtis Granderson and Grady Sizemore, Upton represents a generation sure to provide excitement for years to come.

50 CURTIS GRANDERSON

POSITION: CENTER FIELD
TEAM: DETROIT TIGERS
THROWS: RIGHT
BATS: LEFT
UNIFORM #: 28

Curtis Granderson loves baseball and basketball so much that he played both of them in high school, and he wanted to play both in college, at the University of Illinois-Chicago. But a broken thumb suffered as a sophomore made him focus on baseball full-time. What a lucky break for the Tigers! In 2007, Curtis became just the third Big Leaguer to have 20 home runs, 20 doubles, 20 triples and 20 stolen bases in one season. Nobody in the Majors had done that since Willie Mays in 1957. His example teaches the importance of making the most of your opportunities. Both of Curtis's parents are educators, and that's probably why he started the Grand Kids Foundation, which provides school supplies and books for needy kids and families.

magic number

13

The size shoe Curtis wore in the eighth grade

factoid
For a personal account of Curtis's baseball insights and experiences, check out his ESPN.com blog, where you can read his entries and even write to him.

The BEST Of All Kinds

Can't get enough? There are plenty of baseball bests to keep on debating. Take your pick ...

BEST FASTBALL

a. Joba Chamberlain
b. Jonathan Papelbon ▼
c. J.J. Putz
d. Ben Sheets
e. Justin Verlander

BEST HITTING PITCHER

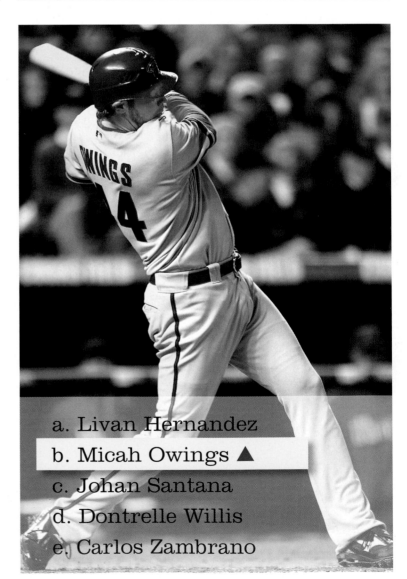

a. Livan Hernandez
b. Micah Owings ▲
c. Johan Santana
d. Dontrelle Willis
e. Carlos Zambrano

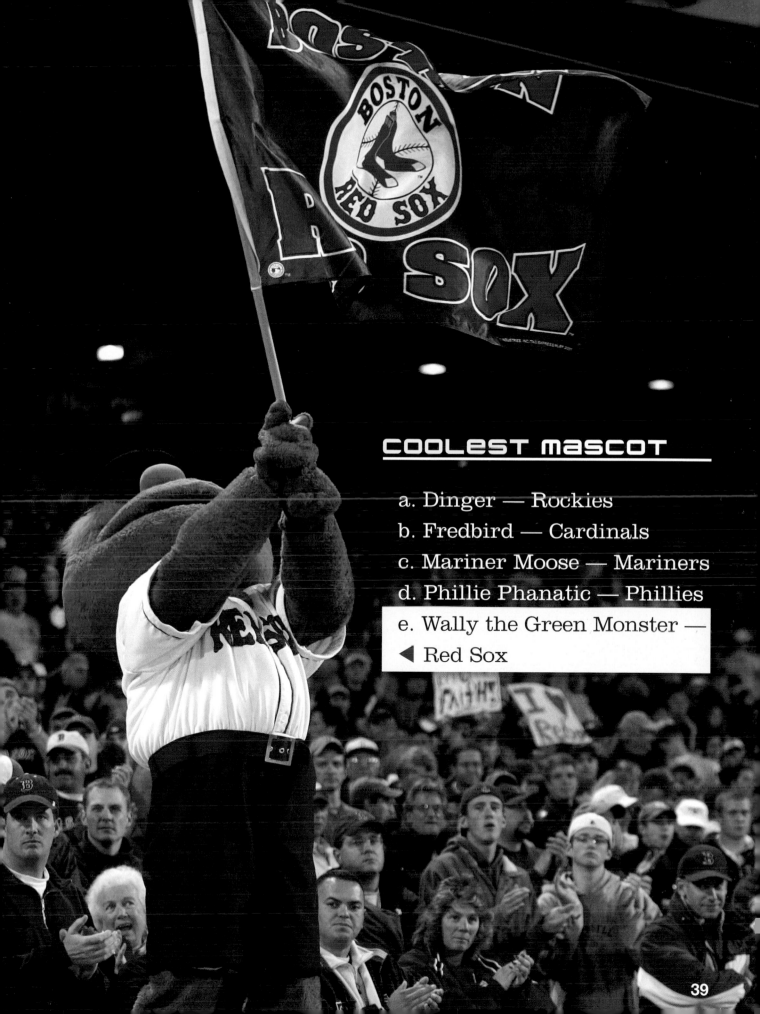

COOLEST MASCOT

a. Dinger — Rockies
b. Fredbird — Cardinals
c. Mariner Moose — Mariners
d. Phillie Phanatic — Phillies
e. Wally the Green Monster —
◀ Red Sox

3 5 5

Best Ballpark Feature

a. The Green Monster — Fenway Park, Boston

b. McCovey Cove — AT&T Park, San Francisco

◀ c. Outfield Ivy — Wrigley Field, Chicago

d. Rays Touch Tank — Tropicana Field, Tampa Bay

e. Riviera Pools Pavilion — Chase Field, Arizona

Scariest Hitter

a. Adam Dunn

b. Prince Fielder

c. David Ortiz ▶

d. Albert Pujols

e. Alex Rodriguez

QUICKEST DOWN THE LINE

a. Jacoby Ellsbury
b. Joey Gathright
c. Carlos Gomez
◀ d. Jose Reyes
e. Ichiro Suzuki

BIGGEST JOKESTER

a. Ken Griffey Jr.
◀ b. Manny Ramirez
c. Jose Reyes
d. Nick Swisher
e. Vernon Wells

BEST WALL CLIMBER

a. Torii Hunter ▲
b. Gary Matthews Jr.
c. Alex Rios
d. Aaron Rowand
e. Grady Sizemore

MOST TOOLS

a. Carlos Beltran ▲
b. Curtis Granderson
c. Alex Rodriguez
d. Grady Sizemore
e. David Wright

BEST EYE AT THE PLATE

a. Bobby Abreu
b. Todd Helton ▶
c. Victor Martinez
d. Manny Ramirez
e. Brian Roberts

PLAYER

Now that you've read all about *The Major League Baseball Best 50*, you can use box scores and stat sheets to keep track of every game and at-bat! Below, you can fill in the

PLAYER	SEASON	AVG	HR	RBI	SB

BATTER TRACKER

TRACKER

statistics for all of your favorite hitters and pitchers. Enter the players' names into the empty spaces, and use the grid to keep an eye on their numbers.

PITCHER TRACKER

PLAYER	SEASON	W/L	ERA	K	SV

fun&games

Nowadays, stats like **OBP** and slugging percentage for hitters and **WHIP** (walks and hits per inning pitched) for pitchers are used more often than batting average or ERA to determine a player's true value. Listed below are the top seven hitters in the Majors in **OPS** (on-base plus slugging percentage) and the top seven starting pitchers in **WHIP** for 2007. Look for their last names in all directions: up, down, backward, forward and diagonal.

```
R  T  E  W  Q  U  R  A  J  N  I  Y  P  A  B
C  O  R  S  A  Y  J  N  Z  S  I  M  T  R  Z
P  R  D  B  J  O  N  E  S  L  K  C  S  W  O
N  T  X  R  Y  U  H  P  Q  H  M  P  H  T  M
O  I  K  J  I  N  S  A  B  C  I  N  O  Z  S
T  Z  I  H  E  G  U  S  H  W  G  E  L  V  U
E  N  B  K  I  U  P  E  A  Q  B  L  M  V
Y  D  S  H  O  R  M  E  N  Z  I  L  I  D  D
X  C  V  A  Z  Q  U  E  Z  H  S  N  D  O  S
D  O  T  M  P  E  G  S  T  B  O  Z  A  D  E
I  Z  A  E  L  H  J  A  P  E  A  V  Y  N  X
R  E  D  L  E  I  F  B  E  D  M  I  C  J  R
E  A  D  S  A  N  T  A  N  A  T  X  G  U  A
W  R  M  U  L  S  W  X  L  R  W  A  S  T  N
U  M  B  S  L  Z  E  N  O  D  R  O  J  K  C
```

BATTERS

(Alex) RODRIGUEZ
(David) ORTIZ
(Carlos) PENA
(Chipper) JONES
(Magglio) ORDONEZ
(Prince) FIELDER
(Matt) HOLLIDAY

PITCHERS

(Jake) PEAVY
(Johan) SANTANA
(Erik) BEDARD
(Chris) YOUNG
(James) SHIELDS
(Cole) HAMELS
(Javier) VAZQUEZ